I0616670

Splendors To Remember

DERRICK HARDING

ISBN:
Softcover (SC): 978-621-434-024-8
Harcover (HC): 978-621-434-025-5

Printed in New York by:

OMNIBOOK CO.
99 Wall Street, Suite 118
New York, NY 10005
USA
+1 202-738-1322
www.omnibookcompany.com

First Edition

For e-book purchase: Kindle on Amazon, Barnes and Noble
Book purchase: Amazon.com, Barnes & Noble, and www.
omnibookcompany.com

Omnibook titles may be purchased in bulk for educational, business, fund-raising, or sales promotional use. For more information please e-mail **info@omnibookcompany.com**

Contents

A Bony Proposition

As an effective church membership ensures its progress

So, bones, sinews and muscle bond to keep the structure of the body firm

As they in supple measures join, to give a man's body its grace and poise

So, attitudes and action of members, cause church to excel or spiritually starve,

And to unfold this proposition, four bones must come to light,

Jaws, and wishes and knucklebones, but chiefs of them are strong backbones.

Now the jaws and tongue are necessary evils,

For apart from supporting the ungrateful belly, they gibber, and grumble

And gossip at will,

They frown, they moan, they groan and dare to complain

And for quasi purpose; the carnal grapevine is ever productive,

Yet, they are not like first cousin the wishbones,

They ever wish and accomplish little

I wish I was rich I would give the church

And when they get the cash, they are absent for a long time

So, for the tenure of their church life, wishbones achieve very little.

They have always been passive and remain this way,

We must pray for them.

Yet aggressive knuckle bones, the assertive ones, target everyone to feed off their energy,

And opposes them with sarcasm and disdain

So those who are knuckles will keep membership in check, like a band around the waist to keep the belly in place.

But of course, there are backbones

They are positive, purpose-drven and full of faith

Backbones are givers; and they are supportive,

You can depend on them to keep the sanctuary open

Yet, some of the times they care little about recognition

And they never blow trumpets to proclaim their intention,

They lead from the front and get the job done.

By Derrick Harding.

Appointment With Disappointment

The love between Mary and Jesus was mutual

He healed her and she was grateful

Her brother Lazarus was sick

And she sent for her confidant.

Jesus delayed for four days, he died

Her world caved in, and hope was dashed

A guaranteed appointment, turned disappointment

If you were here my brother wouldn't have died.

But Jesus had resurrection power.

Derrick Harding

Be Ready

There is jubilee in my heart today

It swells the pleasure of my thoughts

It is the music that I to play,

For I see your presence here,

The mystery of salvation plan…

Men turn from sin by faith and grace,

Estrange from God, they flag in flaw

But love devised a master plan, that those

who were so far from God,

The moment that they fall and call

That hidden perfect, purchase prize

Was fashioned from their dreary life

And surely one day soon they'll rise;

when Christ meets the Church, His faithful bride.

By Derrick Harding

Boepotong Massaeare 1992

Boepotong people, massacred in blood

Slaughtered again in a violent flood

I tell you my brother, I feel your pain

Forty reported, hundreds unknown

Injustice is meted

The treatment unwarranted

Another excuse, White South African choose

To prove their innocence, and justify their wrong,

But the dawn of Democracy on the horizon is poised

And freedom of the Black Man like the phoenix will rise

So brothers be strong; stand firm Boepotong

Apartheid is wounded and mortally too

Soon you will rise as the sphinx, in triumph from your plight,

You'll be masters of your destiny; when South Africa is free.

By Derrick Harding

Divorced(Broken Promises)

The Lily and the rose were inseparably joined

And side by side in their garden grew,

They tended with care this garden fair

And by and by engrafted three

The finest, healthiest, robust buds,

Passersby like bees and birds,

lavished on them, their true delight.

Then one sad day, to her regret

The rose got careless, his petal soiled

And gloom so soon o'er the garden strewed,

With tears of anguish, they sopped their beds

Till by and by the storm was passed.

The lily in turn, broke the golden rule

Not gloom but doom rocked the garden fair

The lily took leave and ne'er returned

That thorns and thistles there feast and spread

and choked the garden until it died.

BY Derrick Harding

Call Out For Help 2

When you are down, don't count yourself out
The delay is short lived; transform your mind
When the last dollar is in your pocket,
You are temporary broke
You can't pay the bills;
Yet your world won't collapse
You are still joint heir with Christ
So call out for help.

Do the foolish thing no one expects
Do it, though it sounds contrary;
Give thanks for what you have,
Praise the Lord if you are in a mess
Cry for help if you fail the test
Cry for help though it cause you grief
And your pain is added strain
Cry for help though it seems in vain
Face your today and hope for tomorrow?
Find your peace in the silence of now;
God's abundant grace is forever free
But you cannot seem to find it;
Look yourself in the mirror; cry one resounding
Yes! For help is on the way.

By Derrick Harding

Compassion

Compassion for the young as aged,

It's not an option lightly choose

But a praxis to revere

This tenet, old, but ever new

Honor parents in the Lord

Bestow long life and child survival

when properly nurtured.

And strong they take the baton of life;

Build a solid nation for posterity

With chaste delight, hang its flag high

Their conscience set them free,

If in love they earn this credit;

They will not spurn the crown

But woe be gone to that nation,

When their best they did not do,

If by choice or sheer neglect, the weak

should suffer, while leaders live as kings.

By Derrick Harding.

Confronting Life

What fearless competitor you are, life!
You exempt none, yet impact all
The rich, the poor, the young and old, the
weak and even the strong
You infect, without mercy,
You ask no question, nor seek permission
Yet you crowd him and snatch his days,
Why do you beguile him of his strength?
You age him, enfeeble him,
Brings him bane and pain
Is there a point to this,
 or just one of your tricks?
It looks like revenge,
sounds like it, so what must I conclude?
You are indeed,
You weigh him down; folks say he looks well,
Yet he cannot see his toes
With a belly of Nine Months
H's crushed
And you express neither regret nor remorse
For seventy years he succumbs to your game
Once, twice over and over until seventy plus
Now I cannot tell you my disappointment
For he dares not make an appeal,
You have neither heart nor soul.

By Derrick Harding

Passions of Autumn

Sweet music of the autumn breeze, speaks the word

That gently calls my scattered thoughts to haste

For every leaf and twig that falls, ignites the passion

I recall

I see them tortured sawn asunder, beaten dipped in

Steaming oil

Yet sweet victory on there faces crown

The martyrs head so proudly worn, that paves

the way and freedom gave, to those who

seek to emulate their feet,

That freedom now we often spurn, yet in the autumn

breeze I find, the truth that so pervade my mind

The harvest fields so white the task, the frontiers

surely dilly waits

The reaping of this wealth so rare

I do know the job is great

For with jaundice eyes the world awaits

For the Sons of God to arise

By Derrick Harding

Wooing Lovers

The bluish waters ripple and gleam
Pink lilies shimmer at the water's edge
April sunlight beams a glorious smile
on emerald leaves matting the inviting waters.
Two young lovers saunter hand in hand, casting
 sticky shadows on the seductive scene
Caressing feet trip on downy green
Gullible hearts flatter joyfully pleased
Two spirits swell with youthful pride,
like ladies skirt ballooning in the cheerful gust,
The wind sweetly echoes and applauses their
dreams, as they mounted castles in stories high.

By Derrick Harding

Do It Now

Move on to your fresh horizon

Hold not to your yesterday's

Let success and failures fly

Like changing shooting stars

Jetting as passing wind

Reach out and seize your shining prize

Don't miss your place but at the top

And take no cushion on your ride

For there is no comfort at the top but

Infinite rooms for excellence

Then be not rigid in your plans

Do not watch the cycle turning

But be responsive none-the-less

And challenge yourself to victory.

By Derrick Harding

My Lady Moon

My Lady Moon I see you tonight
As I blanket myself so cozy and warm
You shimmer, through the quivering leaves
Yet not to do me any harm.

But dear Lady Moon I am not so please
For many, the souls so safe you keep
Have ignored your presence
They are now fast asleep

And oh my dear Lady, there is no one
Who can match the soft sheen, in the light that you beam
I stretch out my hand to touch your soft glow
But the street lamp blinks, that must be jealousy.

For alas dear Lady you are so reliable
And this we concur, with our loved ones and friends
The villages and country sing your joy and praise
For bright lights of the city hide your face.

You are never indifferent but always content, to brighten
dark alleys, where evil will lurk
Concealed in the hedge all but to pounce

On that lonely traveler, a long way from home.
Compassionate as ever, you never forget,
the family awaiting the traveler's return
As a wind quickly whiffs, all the branches just shift
And the rugged old ruffian is put on flight.

By Derrick Harding

Road Accident

The ghastly tale riddles their minds and drains life giving hope

When the tanker accident crashes its scarce commodity,

It bursts in reckless flames, rages havoc and cages future on hold

It sets up boundaries far and wide, cripples mobility and wreathes helpless hands.

Twitching stomachs agonize and repugnantly rave,

The comical hydrant mocks, drips drains, sympathizes,

Yet, withheld its blessings, stifles and frustrates firemen.

Victims trap, resist, scream then succumb to the lapping flames

Pungent gust of seething flesh defuses and wafts upon the breeze

And guilt and doom ravish innocent minds,

And stamp indelibly, a memory bank in gory blood

Road Accident!

By Derrick Harding

Still Love You

Never the less I sing your song

The old but new familiar song

Though you, like thousand abandoned me

Yet my pastures are still green

I suckle you and nurture you,

I gave you all the best of me,

But now?

Yet I will not lament

I am still your fair homeland, robust on

The tropical rock, teeming with the

 Effervescence of faithful life

They are as joyful as in the 1490s

When the ecstatic seaman sounded the alarm:

Land Ahoy!

By Derrick Harding

Great Minds

The truly great mind is as the ocean wide
But deeper yet in its exploits and guile
It rises above vices of arrogance and selfishness,
Liberates the oppressed and comforts the weak
It flushes out corruption, tears down barriers of
Prejudice and reconciles wrongs,
It bridges the gap between the illiterate and
The learned, and plays rich and poor on common
Ground.
It thrives on challenges though mighty or difficult:
The arches through which the great mind succeed.

By Derrick Harding

Man's Destiny

I understand my mortality;

I am a living saint

It is an unchangeable destiny

With no end in sight,

A change from mortal to immortality

will be his final call, that brings perpetual

bliss to those, who heed the master's call.

By Derrick Harding

Not My Will

Provoke me to be broken

The ordinary no longer satisfies

Increase the thermal in your furnace

I submit on your anvil to the hammering

To what you choose

Or turn me on your potter's wheel to the

vessel you desire

I want no part with the loser when the greater

Is all I admire

I will walk with you the extra mile regardless

Of what it takes

By Derrick Harding

Man And Time

Time is sacred but not a secret
Time is precise and faithful in reward
Time cannot be broken,
Time cannot be harnessed or planned
But certainly, we can plan in and on time
Time is and always will be.

Time is a paradox
It is always in motion
Yet time stands still to the naked eye
 But for the natural elements, time is invisible
Time is abundant, yet not enough
Time is always in demand
Always scarce for the busy
And the lazy has all the time in the world
Time waits on no man and passes but once
When squandered and abused we pay dearly.

Time is an expendable resource,
and a most precious commodity
Wasted time is destiny differed.
Time well spent is time spent for God
Time exists for man, not man for time
but man for the times

Man in time is destined,

If a man dies, so is his time

Yet not his times

To him is measured a season

And he must accept without reason

For time is on a journey, that is,

it shall always be eternal.

SELAH

By Derrick Harding

Please Fix It God

You do all the right things
Finite mind can conceive
Yet instead of victory, defeat you receive
You pay your daily sacrifice?
So you think.
But, is your best now in question,
or is your sacrifice in recession?
Your crossroad seems a maze
Uncertainty makes you daze
Is it the past that lingers?
Do you hear it in your spirit?
The broken record that irks;
The pain that has ever been
Yet you clutch it deep within
You guard it with your life.
Is it a grudge, malice or two?
A relationship held dear
That mauls you to despair
Is it a root of bitterness?
The constant turmoil you resist?
That snuffs away your joy.
Does it derail your instant praise?
Like man you rightly scream?

God, are you there!

Well, the news is never better

You are not alone.

Ours may be different

But we've been there at sometime

We have gone to our place of sacrifice

We meet God face to face

Nothing broken stays in his hands

It is His pleasure to fix broken treasure.

By Derrick Harding July5 2008

Blessed Sons

God rehears my life from before I was born

He designs me from an unbelievable master plan

With no back -up but infinite potential

Though I am fearfully and wonderfully made

Every information is classified and secured by the Holy Ghost

I am a classic example of God's foolproof security, hidden

with Christ in Him

He is familiar with every micro millimeter of my frame

And is intimate with every billion of each cell, thought and

interest of my life

He examines every idea and motive before they become action

He justifies the falling of every hair and replaces every dead cell

God makes me in his righteousness

I sit in heavenly places; feast on the bread of life

Drink from the fountain of lining water

God grants me every spiritual blessings in heavenly places

And I readily partake of everything pertains to life and godliness

I can do all things through Christ who strengthens me

As he supplies all my needs according to his riches in glory by Christ

Therefore I have nothing broken, nothing missing and I have no lack.

By Derrick Harding

Happy Valentines

And I wish to tell you darling
You mean so much to me
You are at the center of my universe
And he future in my dreams
I love our times together
The moments that we share,
The things you do to tell me
My darling I do care
I wish you joy and happiness
I wish you love sublime
I wish that you will always
Be as lovely as you are
And on every day in every way
Be my very, special friend

By Derrick Harding

Curfew

Curfew again mi freedom done
Sojaman cum wid'im big shot gun
Im bus some shots, dem scare the dead
A tell yu sah, de man dem dread.
Sojaman comb, every house under siege
Whole night dem raze de unity achieve
Kick it up, mash it up, beat it to pulp
Till dawn of day, Kaaz non takin na gwan.
A tell you sah the man dem dread.
Destruction grim in the rising sun
Fi si the wase, fi sojaman fun
Wilted spirits huddled in a bundle
Picture this, distress, aganizing in pain
Kaan scratch, kaan bend, han pon dem head.
Heaven knows this, di man dem dread
Total devastation of families integrity
Brutal destruction of dem faith in the system
Tried, convicted, condemned before justice
Punished without mercy for two spent shells
Detainees swell.
All eyes black and blue, dem self-esteem bruise.
Mi sa mi tell you sah, the man dem dread

Ruthless injustice rife everywhere
Excused by law, a legislative flaw
Johny han bruk, Jerry head bus
Everybody a wait fi Black Maria fi come.
So yu si mi tell you, sah, di man dem dread.

By Derrick Harding

Dad's Special Day

We recognize you this special day

To tell you all the niceties, we miss out during the year

And dad, I know you are not the one, to make a fuss about these things

But I saw you this morning how happy you were, as you got ready for church

You came all dressed up, looking smart, so I know this day belongs to you

And I must tell you, that whiff of cologne,

My, my, my, it smells so good

you took such care, to fix your tie, and placed ever strand of hair

And I must confess, if you allow them to grow like mine, you will look even smarter

But put fun and joke aside, there are some things I must tell you,

I remember the early days, you use to take me on your lap; you read to me a lot.

I love the stories you read at nights then prayed Lord's Prayer

I could depend on you, to show up for ball practice, just when it mattered most.

I remember the day I fell, I was bruised all over but you loved me with such tender care.

Your sense of loyalty, honesty and kindness make me want to be like you

The way you care about my Mom, It means a lot to me.

Now that I am growing up, I sure would like to be just like you.

I like when we all come to church

Mom says, she would have it no other way.

But dad I am worried about one thing

if we die now, would we all go to heaven?

I know that Mom and I are Christians

My Sunday school teacher tells me, hell is an awful place;

but Jesus died to prevent us from going there

So Dad, if you die today do you know where you will go?

Derrick Harding

I Hear Grandma Pray

Enough is enough, she firmly says

The uproar which follows, I 'll not forget.

This vision here, I now relate

Enough is enough, she firmly whispers

The effect sends off mighty rumbling

Windows brake and doors went tumbling

Voices echo and footsteps stamping

Compel to run, but I know the drill

I wait to see the ruinous fate …

'The Bull in the Chinese's shop;'

Or is it a grenade thrown,

Curiosity holds me spell bound

Startled indeed, the comedy brakes

My tears and laughter mingled sweet

Ma is praying and that is sweet

Her punch line is so deadly, who wouldn't laugh?

My children, grandchildren my great

Grandchildren you will not have

And naturally, I joined the chant

My children, grandchildren my great

Grand children you will not have

I watch her tear stained face

I smell her delicate Johnsons Baby powder

And a lump wells up in my throat

She is barely young, at ninety
But she packs a deadly punch
To mastermind the destructive plan
Thousands of demons who explode in terror
are no match for this feeble saint
Enough is enough.
For though she is one,
There are four that lead the charge.

By Derrick Harding.

The Times Of Man

The times of man shall last forever

Those of darkness, light or silence

Personal joys and loathsome sorrows

Gain or loss came in blessing shower

To crystallize one lasting treasure

or

In priceless pleasure or hopeless rejection:

The times of man that live-forever.

By Derrick Harding

Faith Empowered

I was diagnosed with Leukemia February 3, 2014.

I showed no signs nor symptoms.

It has been the best days of my life,

May be I don't actually mean that

But it is the time I felt most alive and conscious about my faith

I spent very little money, had a massive medical procedure,

I was healed and empowered.

Faith, has empowered me to see life in a different way

I focused more on God to change my situation

I had several vivid conformation that I would be healed

I realized that sickness and life never always make faith easy

But I published a book which recounted the ordeal

This will strengthen the faith of those who are struggling with illness.

Those whose lives are ravaged with doubts, fear and disappointment

should read and meditate on these inspired words.

By Derrick Harding

Forgiveness

That passion prevails

He prostrate on his face

God, is in control

He must seek the truth

The truth that avenges this wrong

His faith is waning; his anger burns

The blatant facts he never spurns

His spirit craves for something more

Stricken with fear he grieves in pain

Is she in another man's arm!

Then who must die?

His tear-stained face just tells the tale

Oh God, You know he loves her still!

But how can he forgive this wrong?

He weeps, he prays and intercedes

As conscience whips him into to shame

It rides him till repentance came,

Then in that moment of conception

God's love favor his redemption

He forgives and he finds peace.

By Derrick Harding

Frightened Child

If I can but this moment touch, the yearning
spirit deep within your troubled heart
succor the ice-cold fear of your guarded stare,
uncover the imprisoned joy stifled beneath
your breathing
Then, I will cherish this moment ever,
Your sunbeam smile speaks to the peace my
conscience seeks.

Derrick Harding

Infallible God Genuine Message.

God transcends the universe and all material things

That means He could stand independent of all

and present a perfect- salvation to an imperfect world

That the salvation of God is genuine

Therefore, in the present case, Gamali, in The Book of Acts, advise:

"--------------you leave these men alone! Let them go!

For if their purpose or activity is of human origin, it will fail.

But if it is from God, you will not be able to stop these men;

you will only find yourselves fighting against God."

Hence Jesus died to make salvation possible

And, we strive to make it available.

To make salvation available demands the preaching

of a genuine message, that is global diverse and all= inclusive

A genuine message brings genuine converts.

Genuine converts become genuine worshipers who

are giving, loving and kindhearted

By Derrick Harding

Happy Valentine

And I wish to tell you darling
You mean so much to me
You are at the center of my universe
 The future in my dreams
I love our times together
The moments that we share,
The things you do to tell me
My darling I do care;
I wish you joy and happiness
I wish you love sublime
I wish that you will always
be, as lovely as you are
And on every day in every way
Be my very, special Valentine.

By Derrick Harding

Militant For Christ

Your strain is my pain, we war in the Spirit

Within our hearts we firmly unite

We dare not relent,

We'll face every woe, and challenge every foe

We'll march on together

We'll stand in the gap

We'll fight and we'll conquer,

in this spiritual war

we'll forge this this fight together

No band aid solution

can camouflage our resolve

We bear our souls

With fire in our guts

We'll blast them thus

In the face of despair,

Every man is riled up

The Savior gives the writ,

The Holy Spirit, the queue

We take authority over self,

And the evil of their defense

Is in subjection to our obedience

We'll display in this conference the awesomeness of your faith

Every weapon formed; every violent intent,

Must suffer from the hand of our vengeance
We are strong at the front,
With Jesus is our general
We stand to make a difference
for the sake of the Kingdom.

By Derrick Harding

Henry Wadsworth Longfellow

The heights by great men reached and kept

Were not attained by sudden flight;

But they, while their companions slept,

Were toiling upward through the night -

Hope My Little Ones

Hope my child,

My little one

Dearest, warmest, lovely face

Pleasant as the morning sunbeam

Rejoices my pulsating heart

To witness, the warmth and aura of your smiles

And the sparkle of your ivory teeth

Confirms the blessings of heaven's best

Yet timid, frightful fledgling,

You crave of me the question

So sad, too sad my little ones

That crime of selfishness today, is eating at

your soul, even as I pray for you,

But, there is hope, perfect hope my little ones

There is nothing now that troubles you

that Jesus never, ever knows

So live your dream, in him confide

And share his blessings everyday.

By Derrick Harding

Crazy Society – St. Mark 5 Legion

You stilt think I am crazy

But, am I a mad man?

You'd better hold that perception

of your distorted vision

Look on me again and see.

I am not mad

I am only hungry

Couldn't you see that?

Am I too alive to be dead?

or too dead in your eyes

I was lonely

You never hugged me

In chains, you never loose them

You misunderstand my

plea, how odd for a Christian!

Now Christ has set my record straight

The past He totally takes away

Yet my presence knocks you flat,

Now I am in awe, total awe,

That even in this honored place

You still cannot accept me.

By Derrick Harding

Tribute To Mama

Today we celebrate a life well lived
Unselfish devoted and lovingly gave
To nurture the lives of scores you know,
Today we celebrate with tears of joy
Un matchless divine, is the hope we share
For the life you loved and held so dear
Is resting now in the Savior's arms
The pearly gates were opened wide
And angels took her on their fight
The choirs of heaven
Sang sweetest praise
Now there is hope for you and me
to join her when the Savior calls.

By derrick Harding

First Encounter

It was an early August morning
I was still but very young
I lay awoke unhappily
My fearful thoughts swirled in my head,
And my heart went pounding in my bed;
I saw a light as the curtain drew
My mother had marked this decisive hour,
I heard her voice spoke tenderly
My son come let me pray with you.
Released from my bed of sheer distress,
I walked with her to the living-bed room.
Mast Der, her tender voice appealed
Something is happening in your heart,
I felt a lump gulped in my throat
And tears came streaming down my face,
It is called conviction son,
Jesus wants to come into your heart
Now I remember that decisive hour,
my first encounter with the Lord.

By Derrick Harding

How Are You Dressed?

Are you functioning in a full proof armor

The one That does not work for you?

Though it works for evangelist

For them who preach a social gospel

That does not address sin

Why would you run with horses when foot men are desperate?

You feed them on milk, how about strong meat

David did not run contrary to the dictates of his heart

He served a menial task, just carried lunch for his brothers

Yet he became a mighty man of valor.

Saul could not wear his own armor to fight Goliath

Yet he dressed David to match the eight hundred pounds armored giant

David did not test his armor, he resorted to the ordinary full proof; A sling and stone.

Plus the invisible armor of God.

By Derrick Harding

I Am Still Standing

You cannot keep a blessed man down

Though you slay, you knocked him flat

Yet he will rise like the statue of Liberty

Hand point toward the sky,

And the Negro Arose his face toward the golden sun

Yet shall he rise

You throw at him everything you got, nearly to the end of his life

You slap Leukemia on him, when he showed no signs or symptoms

You stage a fall when he was weak from chemotherapy

At your liberty you busted his left carotid artery

You thought that he would die

You compounded it with a massive aneurysm

Pain became his close companion

Yes he should have died but he is still standing, but for the grace of God

The undisputed, infallible, imperishable word of God was never in doubt.

By Derrick Harding

I Speak To The Sons Of God

I speak to all men but not for all

The harvest field is ready white

But not all men can see without you patting

them on the back and point out the obvious

Although a storm is looming low, they

continue to kick the can down the track

Therefore, I speak to men indeed

Men who must change the world

I speak to men of integrity,

Men whose wealth belongs to God

Men whose passion burns in their guts

Men who will fulfill God's agenda,

Therefore I speak to men of purpose,

Men who fast without the mask

I speak to men who refuse to quit

I speak to men, who whose strength is in Christ,

Men who believe in the impossible

The power of the word is their compass

I speak to unwavering men of faith,

I speak to men who know they are called

Can I speak to men with passion for the vision?

Can I challenge some conscious men; men whose

Righteousness is in Christ

Can I challenge those men, crucified with Christ?

who will live by faith in the Son of God

Can I challenge real men?

May I challenge the Sons of God, Sons who rise will up like
Joseph, defied Potiphar's wife, exalted in Egypt and reign victorious
May I challenge the Joshua gang who saw themselves
as the giant and the Philistines as grasshoppers.
May I call forth Daniel, and David and Paul, who will take the
Sword of the Spirit in their hand: unmoved like Steven, dying, but
Declaring, "Father, do not charge them for this sin."
Is there even one Son, armored and ready to assault
the Kingdom of darkness?
May I tell that Son, that he is called to the kingdom
for such a time as this.

By Derrick Harding

Life In Perspective/Death &Dying

Death is a comma in the sentence of life.

As the dash is your lifespan

The former allows you to focus and reflect on your life's account,

And the latter, that of one who passes away

Reflection brings eternity in sharp focus

You like the one who dies is destined to face eternity

The dash however, reveals your hopes, dreams and aspirations

As well as failure and Triumphs,

Consequently, though you will decide for eternity.,

For spurning the opportunity, you remain lost.

By Derrick Harding

Militant For Christ

Your strain is my pain, when we war in the Spirit

Deep within our hearts we are firmly united

We dare not relent,

We'll face every woe, and challenge every foe

We'll march on together

We'll stand in the gap

We'll fight and we'll conquer,

in this spiritual war

When we dare to unite

Forge together in this fight

No band aid solution, can camouflage our resolve

We bare our souls.

There is fire in our guts

We spill thus

We dare to be bold, in the face of despair,

Every man is riled up

For the Savior gives the writ,

The Holy Spirit gives the queue

Take authority over self, every ploy or pretence,

Every evil of their defense

Is in subjection at this conference

Every weapon that is formed; and every violent intent,

Must be subject to our vengeance when our obedience is fulfilled

We are brothers at the front, united, as we are blunt
Judge no man, but we bless everyone,
We are brothers on a mission, with Jesus as our general
We stand to make a difference
just for the sake of the Kingdom of God.

By Derrick Harding

Man In Crisis

Man, stop marginalize yourself

Wake up to the truth for the die is cast

The ball is squarely in your court

Rise up man and recognize your plight

Claim by faith your Godly heritage

You have a gender issue that is not right

Stem the tide and stop the slide

Enough of your inept conceit,

Rise up man and take a stand

Grasp fleeting destiny in your hand.

Too long Slip Willy, you vacate your role?

You let your woman pay the dole.

Now you think she threatens your place

You'll wish to God that you were dead

Man, stop cowering before your gender price

Get up off your corner and find your niche

Give yourself a fighting chance

Be the kind of man you ought to be, a good

father and a caring man,

Assert yourself, wear the pants

And be a man if you think you can.

By Derrick Harding

Migration

What do you have at stake?

Is it material things?

Is it the memory of the choices you made?

Have they followed your life?

Isn't it more to leaving

When you pick and pack two cases of seventy pounds

Then you question,

Is this all you worth?

After all, there is fun and fanfare

The good byes and good luck are emotive

As a bird in a storm you become a captive in flight

And all that you have is the reality of your thoughts

Maybe peace, joy, confusion or I don't care one bit

You left all else behind

But when all is done, there is one question you must answer

Have you fulfilled your purpose in the lives you left behind?

By Derrick Harding

Missed Opportunity

You stir my heart so very much

In ways it has never been before

You weakened every joint in me;

when I saw your smile, every nerve in me vibrate.

I could not resist the thought, I felt

I had to hear that lovely name,

And when you spoke, I melt inside

It was ecstatic

But I fell straight back to earth;

You said I could not call.

By Derrick Harding

Morning Guest

What joy to him her entrance brings
But out of obligation follows protocol,
Two thousand eyes are looking on
Fix him adhesively to his chair
And as he watches, she lightly flits,
She perches a daring hand breadth away.

All gaze from eyes of mutual fun
The Quit ignores the faces,
So he bows his head to her
"Good morning little one,"
In turn, surprisingly,
She flits her tail. She does a jig.

"Good morning little birdie,"
He chances again,
She hails to him a squeaky sound,
And this I know you rightly guess,
His boyish joy over flows and starts
The audience visibly trembles with stitches
Some dab their eyes to hide the tears.
He sits erect and fixes his tie.
He is a teacher don't you forget.

By Derrick Harding

My Country Groans

(Jamaica's walk from Independence to October 2002)

My country groans, but I must hope,

That one day soon our best will thrive

so we can never be at ease, until this blessing we achieve

Our fathers dream; all fact is fact

Our young men too no vision lack

But in indiscipline, we still mope

for we are just but selfish folks.

With tension and strife the nation is rife,

Spiritually blind, we grope in darkness

We are wasteful and rough, as indignant and proud

That's an awful receipt for growth

Hence for this cause, my country groans. ??

Childhood then, in the sixties dawn

And, we all rest on bead of easy

The economy is safe we all agree

But colonial rules we all embrace

Yet still, for inexperience, my country groans.

But the seventies rise, energetic teen thrives

The turbulent youth of wisdom scarce, rises to a

crescendo with the crackle popping lash,

Western ideals we flatly eschew

With gusto and rhetoric, we blast right-wingers wild
Fortune and talent escape by flight
in visions dreams we lament our plight
So with growing pains, my country groans.

Yet manhood blooms in the eighties soon,
And garners strength and hope to build
But oil prices and the dollar sky
Black market strive and foreign stuff arrive
Selfhood despairs and backs away
So you see why my country groans.

Yet the nineties come; fresh challenges loom
The dollar hiccups, and winces and slides
One million gems glitter, bids us wait
All so deception, we agape with awe
Yet, the dollar held firm in temporary respite
But the symbolic giant was never mutual
The nation flinches, but rolls with the punches
The Road to France brings needed distractions
So the Olympic gold cushions the blows
Yet a third term, poses more than questions,
So fate has its way, and my country groans.
Hard to believe that we have not learned the secret of life
In 1962 crime rate was 3.9% per 100,000
Since 1970 to 2011 crime and violence skyrocketed.

Since 2012 there is no description to fit the bill,
Speak of Yardies, Jamaican posse and crime now against LGBT
Therefore I must agree this is no receipt for growth,
when you are 6th on the Murder list worldwide
(Un report April 11,2014)
 So what need I say, O Lord my country groans.

By Derrick Harding

Mystic Muse

The mystery of joy divine

Caress my heart in comfort sweet

The peace I sought relentlessly

Now quiets my heart with thankfulness

For the love I yearn, now warms

my heart forever.

By Derrick Harding

The Nightingale"S Symphony

It was a September morning

When I heard her sweetly singing

She sang to me distinctly from the

bowers of a towering cedar tree

I sipped her gracious words;

They reminded me of my childhood

It was a pleasure to recall

I listened, I heard

She sang some more

A sweeter tune she never played

A beautiful morn, a beautiful mourn

A beautiful morning I thought I heard

Allegretto more than allegro but

a symphony all its own

I shivered down my spine, and squirted

saliva in my jaws

My soul at last was satisfied

My heart in me rejoiced

Breathtaking, life had come to me

In just that simple tune

I gazed up to the top-most branches

Then to the clear blue sky

I got a glimpse of the angelic chic

And just when fortune smiled upon me

Heaven's joy was all I know
She resisted the laws of gravity
I strained my eyes; she soared
My heart was filled with pleasure,
And I whistled her tune long after
she was gone.

By Derrick Harding.

The Christian's Destiny

I understand my mortality;

I am a living saint

Yet, it is an unchangeable destiny

There is no end in sight, for those who heed

the Masters voice

The transfer from mortal to immortality

will be his final call.

By Derrick Harding

Not My Will

Provoke me to be broken

The ordinary no longer satisfies

Increase the thermostat of your furnace

I submit on your anvil

For the hammering that you choose

Or turn me on your potter's wheel to be the
vessel you desire

I want no part with losing,

The greater is all I admire

I will walk with you the extra mile, regardless
of what it requires.

By Derrick Harding

Public Outrage

HE was tried by a cop,

Over -looked by the law

and died by the gun

Unhindered a mother wept,

Consumed with rage, she curled up

and told her story to the world

I heard her plead I heard her sigh

injustice? Does anyone care?

Today I am a victim

The poor has no voice

Crowds gathered; they swore they cursed

They were all enraged, for that life could be theirs

She blamed the system

They shot the innocent mute?

A claim no mortal could refute

He was always a peaceful lad

No previous record, just a harmless smile

Yet he attacked with a piece of plank?

The evidence never came to light

He died in cold blood, a bullet to the head.

By Derrick Harding

Reaching Out

In this broken home do not let me feel deprive
Your sustaining grace will be my guide
Let the earnest spirit of your love radiates through
my anxious heart,
Set me free from the perils of negative thoughts
And fill uncertain hours, that I may rise above the
the calamities of self-indulgence,
Just keep me at bay from their crushing blows,
And secure me from their dreadful woes
Oh Eternal Father, comfort true my aching heart
Put at rest the pounding in my head as I relax upon my bed
Dear God of this family, creator of this fragile home, if there
is a purpose for grinding us through this churn?
Then let the wisdom learned from this pain, and the trial of this
ordeal, be the lesson I will teach,
Let them be the beacon in the darkest hours for some hurting
Family, struggling on the brink of disaster.

By Derrick Harding

Refuting The Law Of Average.

You are exclusively executive

You are bought with an imperishable seed of excellence

To produce like kind fruit of lasting value.

God's word shall not return to Him void

So, despite your circumstances and limitation,

Your success is never in doubt

God has given you the ability to acquire wealth

Your DNA is rooted in the father

He gives you dominion to rule and subdue

Your ability to propagate is rooted in the word of God

IIs not a matter if you will produce but when and how much,

Christ works by the power and limitation you put on Him

Your production will only dry up when you ceased to provide vessels.

By Derrick Harding

Memories Of Childhood

HOW my latent passion stirs

When childhood memories mirror shine

Treasures of my cohorts come zooming, right

before my very eyes

Loud-mouthed, screaming, lively boys, practice

their serious art of play, without a trace of levity

And what a joy I can recall, of knuckling marbles

and spinning tops, with deft precision, from dexterous hands,

Then pushing, and shoving and bumping heads,

We scramble in a tested line

Now UN your marks, and get set, go!

We dash and dare down the precipitous hill

And unknown records came tumbling down,

But most of all, our reckless, rocketing down

Slick-brown grassy slopes on coconut bough

When holiday gifts of summer peaks

And landing in a crumpled heap, we scream we laugh

Unmatched with joy

For victory crowns our life and play.

By Derrick Harding

Sacrifice What You Have In Your Hand.

Shamgar had an ok goad, David had a sling, Dorcas had a needle
Aaron had a rod, Samson had a jawbone Mary had some ointment,
but they all were used for God.
Therefore, the question to you is: Do you want to succeed?
Then offer to God what you have in your hand as a sacrifice
God does not ask you to create something spectacular with your hand
Though it may come to that
Nor does He ask you to purchase something to use
though you may have to find resources
Moses was a babbler but he had a rod, Solomon had wisdom,
Paul had the word of God in his mouth, but Peter had his boat.
The Zarephath Widow Woman had only a handful
of flour in a jar and a little oil in a jug, but she became a great
entrepreneur and business woman like the boy with the
five loaves and two fishes. So, what do you have in your hand?
Something you have personally, your astute mind, a weapon,
a prize possession, leadership skills, writing ability,
your singing voice or great faith.
if you sacrifice it to God He take what you have, use it for His glory
    and expansion of this kingdom.

By Derrick Harding

She Comes To Stay

Shall I confess that I am excited
I'm walking on celestial air?
I'm lovingly, and joyfully waiting
I dare you to compare
For there is none from far or near
Unless surfeiting with such joy,
can flair the ecstasy that I know.
Every fiber of my being exudes
the music deep within my heart
The song no angel voice can sing
The tears of joy so sweet so dear, are
heaven's blessings from above,
Yet there is a joy I cannot speak,
There is a song I cannot sing
It's music sweet beyond compare
Like nightingale's beauty on early morn
I dare to say no human craft, can share
the beauty of my heart, for my Honey comes to stay.

By Derrick Harding

Side With The Devil

Her frail willowy frame quakes at every lash

of their flagrant tongue,

Her eyes bulge, tears well, brim, and wet her cheeks

Her quivering lips could not defend

For by each volley they compelled submission,

She'll stay clear of teachers' lounge

For not one, not two nor three, but four trouncing

Spanish tongues dose her well.

I raged inside, yet I fail to give her my shoulder.

By Derrick Harding

Spiritual Intercourse

I let the burning passion within my heart draw me behind the inner
  vale

As I strive in desperate need;

Convection prostrates me before the glorified Lord;

I defy nature's calls, I resists detractors

My spirit craves His, during the waking hours

My eyes burn for lack of sleep

I reach out for that one single moment of favor

For the essence of God's magnificence to blanket me…..

To cover me with his Holiness;

And O, the joy that sweeps over me

As He immerses me in His love

I weep, I pray as I intercede

Until I break under the convection that He loves me still

And hope brightens my life that moment, fusing my yes with His,

Then comes one blissful spell of consecration, and I rise pregnant
  with His Seed.

Derrick Harding.

Splendors To Remember

Guilty is the verdict, common sense, his judge

Experiences of his past, he never

 brought to life

Carelessness or sheer neglect,

The reason he can't recall

Ideas glowing in his mind,

were treated as rejects

His conscience now awakens

His heart with guilt overflows

He moves with desperation

To walk away from lazy folks,

that refuse to assert themselves,

And by default, has come to buy, his very ideas,

from another man's print

And so, his passion is set a blazed

He gropes on his psychic shelves,

He wrestled from the thief of mind,

ideas curtained as rejects, he never might recall,

Creates he gems of lasting treasures.

Those he garners, polishes and preserves

Ideas old but ever new

become shining splendors to remember.

By Derrick Harding

Stopping By Woods On A Snowy Evening

Adapted by Robert Frost

Whose woods these are I think I know.
His house is in the village, though;
He will not see me stopping here
To watch his woods fill up with snow.
My little horse must think it queer 5
To stop without a farmhouse near
Between the woods and frozen lake
The darkest evening of the year.
He gives his harness bells a shake
To ask if there is some mistake. 10
The only other sounds the sweep
Of easy wind and downy flake.
The woods are lovely, dark and deep,
But I have promises to keep,
And miles to go before I sleep,
And miles to go before I sleep.

Sweet Sixteen

You stepped into my path last night
Under the dim fluorescent light
And O, my throbbing heart was glad.
I unveiled you under purple light,
And saw your eyes like angel's bright
I whispered softly in your ears
And your blushing eyes melted with tears.

By Derrick Harding

The Axing

Ah mighty word, cast a light into my darkened cell

Let me see through my tangled thoughts

why this injustice is so crowned

Isn't there another way to do this?

A reprimand, suspension from duty, but why axe him?

How can I understand this coldness I see?

This vintage tree cut down, in the budding of spring

And though I know he will not die, but grow up in some verdant
pasture

I cannot help, for I am sad,

I did not hear an announcement

We regret your hasty departure,

Then how can I agree with the verdict of this case?

Is this blatant unconcern, revenge or just for self-glory?

Are there some heads to roll?

This does not confirm the boast of teamwork,

It is just a puny farce that entertains petty ego

that will lead to the demise of the company.

The fact is this prophesy came to pass.

By Derrick Harding

The Battle Of The Mind.

There is a battle raging in the mind of Christians and the church.

It has nothing to do with politics, though it uses it as a conduit

It has little to do with nuclear devices, nor mass bombing

and mass killing yet it impinges on same on the mind

But it is a diabolic spirit from hell orchestrated by the devil

to control the mind of all those who profess to be Christian.

It is built on fear.

This intense or strong emotion has a paralyzing effect on the

Minds of Christian and the Church.

We adapt the attitude of flight or fight to deal with it,

while none is a perfect substitute.

The devil by creating middle eastern wars and catastrophic,

Events of mass shooting in America, and wars and rumors of wars

Across the globe is to cause fear to cripple the mind.

When he cripples the mind, he cripples the body.

People become anxious, depressed and confused.

We can't think soberly and righteously in this present world.

We can't rightly divide the word of truth, so it is easy for him

to sell a six for a nine.

This is the battle for the mind but your soul.

His interest is in our souls

Though in all these things we are more than conquers through Christ

we have but one recourse in the words of our Lord and mentor

"Thy faith has made the whole."

By Derrick Harding.

The Blessed Sons

God knew my life from before I was born

He designed me from unique master plan

with back up reserves of infinite potential

 I am creatively and beautifully designed

Every information is classified and secured

The Holy Ghost watches and is ever charge

I am classic, foolproof in His security,

hidden in Christ and Christ in God

They are familiar with every micro millimeter of my frame

And are intimate with every billionth of each cell, thought and my
   intentions

He examines every idea and motive before they become action

He justifies the falling of every hair and replaces each dead cell,

My God makes me his righteousness

I sit in heavenly places;

I feast on the bread of life

I drink from the fountain of lining water

God grants me every spiritual blessing in heavenly places

And I readily partake of things pertain to life and godliness

I can do all things for Christ strengthens me

He supplies all my needs with grace from His glory

Therefore, on the whole, I have no lack.

By Derrick Harding

The Dance

You hear the instant drum beat,

You heart feels the tug of pulsating music

You reach out, You see

Her body replies to the enchanting rhythm

She, sways, contorts and defies gravity,

You hear your heart pumping

It throbs in your ears

Instantly, you make connection

Your spirits are inseparable

You see history in her motion

You hear ancestral applause

Their faces set in expectant approval

They will her on to glory

For they see in her their freedom

This dance is but a nugget

Of what life will be,

A nugget for her daily sacrifice

That's why she remains on stage

She sees freedom, that's why toils on.

By Derrick Harding
11/22/03

The Fate Of Three - Fingered Jack

This cad in history is very bold
Three- finger- Jack is his pseudonym
He is not related to Mr. Sprat, nor the ass
for that matter
Yet the man is amazingly strong, and robustly
built as he is tall
His hands and legs are iron bands
His face is long, and thin and tall
with canine teeth for the toughest bones.

This Jack reigns for very long
Fearlessness is his horrific game
He wilds his foe with just one stare
Like his descendants, societies fear,
As dreaded men they come to show
The seed from Jack they strongly bear.

They are in no way the same as he,
Their bullet-riddled bodies do attest
They couldn't trust the penal code
Yes, they are dread, but death is kind
By apt measures societies find.

Surely by now you do remember some
Natty and Henry of the of the Morgan's Clan
And Sanduz of the dreaded Con
Like forefather Jack, protested and died
But who knows the roll of fate
They may rise in elements society abhors.

For the poor are oppressed; injustice is brazened,
flourish on rhetoric and empty promises
That insight resistance in a nation backslidden
And marches and talk shows as good as they are
Will not turn back the impending fury of the
descendants of Three-fingered Jack.

By Derrick Harding

The Forgiven Heart

I hear the music of the heart, chiming
sweetly triumphant sings
It is the language of the soul, spoken only
by the inner man;
When the beauty of the thankful heart unfolds
The inner birth of spiritual love, that tempers
painful bitter scars, indelible itched on the forgiven heart
But replace when pride and hurt shall crumble
on the anvil of the Savior's word
Then thankful hearts which understand, the blessings
of mercy, grace and peace
Their rapturous praise unfold with joy
to testify of the Savior's love.

By Derrick Harding

The God Who Knows

Isn't there a God who cares when your best effort fails?

When you are force to walk under strain and every

practical reason says you must run

Walking keeps you from fainting, when you are pressed to the limit

You crash headlong into the wall that mars your soul

Yet this is not in your plan

Isn't there a God who cares?

Isn't there a God who sees your dream?

That secret quest you share

The quest, that makes you care

That simple innocent joy you crave

The joy that gives you steadfast hope

The joy that makes you want to cope

Yet you watch this mighty triumph slips, even before

you have time to speak

You are brought to your knees; your tears are your meat

Then tell me, isn't there a God who sees?

Isn't there a God who knows your limitless potential in trusting?

A God who knows your every need

A God who knows your faith in deed

A God who listens to your prayers and wipes your falling tears
Yet in all his wisdom he allows your daring test
He must prove you at your best, though you see the worse
When you think your best fails, isn't there a God who knows?

By Derrick Harding

Teachers, (The Honorary Poor)

It is a cruel act, though scholarly the thesis seems
One cannot but observe the irony of the flaw,
Dividing men in classes!
In perception, is t blatantly mean;
If you try hard, you may justify three,
Though, commonsense, sees two; rich and the poor
Or better yet, the haves and the have not
But look beyond the realm of this possibility
For like an ominous cloud, observe this discontent:
An economic witticism, a nondescript....
One comical class has immerges?
I pray your pardon, if it may seem too bold
For Karl Marks or his mentor Engels
Fail to define the status this contrives,
So of interest to this cause, a maxim I shall coin,
And since a name must to be given, do bear with my
simplicity, if I call them "The Honorary Poor"
For it shall be the norm in years to come
And not just an adage of comical repute
For these are people who hail from the Working class,

Professionals, excuse me,
They earn above the minimum wage,
Yet, too poor to buy bread or chicken meat at will
And much too rich to be qualified for food stamps;
But you may observe, they are an extremely ambitious sect

Who do not fit in Karl's Middle Class,

Not just because of the weight of the dollar,

But some, a bit short on principle of banding their belly;

Have spent their monthly salary before they receive the check;

Yet, I pray your sympathy for them,

They are meticulous in budgeting

They excel in pinching scarce resources,

But regardless of how they try, they cannot compete

With the spiraling price increases;

Yet, a hardy bunch, I know they will survive.

By Derrick Harding
(The oil crisis, Jamaica 1973-1974)

The Moon Is Up

Adapted by Alfred Noyes

The moon is up, the stars are bright.
the wind is fresh and free!
We're out to seek the gold tonight!
The world is growing grey and old:
break out the sails again!
We're out to see a Realm of Gold
beyond the Spanish Main.
We're sick of all the cringing knees,
the courtly smiles and lies
God, let Thy singing channel breeze
lighten our hearts and eyes!
Let love no more be bought and sold
for earthly loss or gain;
We're out to seek an Age of Gold
beyond the Spanish Main.

Beyond the light of far Cathay,
beyond all mortal dreams,
Beyond the reach of night and day
Our El Dorado gleams,
Revealing - as the skies unfold -
A star without a stain,
The Glory of the Gates of Gold
beyond the Spanish Main.

The New Frontier

A bold new future looms,

The field is critically white,

It is ready bursting at the seams,

I hear the jubilation cries

Thousands committed voices sing

Tears of sorrow and sweet redemption

Regrets and tears, they wasted time

But joy for mercy full of grace

The Sons of God have come of age

These chew tough meat, digest the word

They need no milk but warfare swords

They come to the kingdom, driven by purpose

To accept their rights; not flinching in plight

To fight and succeed where others failed

They chart new boundaries for the harvest fields.

For militant thousands of exploring conquerors.

By Derrick Harding

The Nightingale's Symphony

It was a September morning

I heard her sweetest song

She sang to me distinctly

I drank her gracious words

They reminded me of childhood

It was a pleasure to recall

I listened, I heard

She sang some more

A sweeter music I have never heard

A beautiful morn, a beautiful mourn

were the word I thought I heard

It was more allegretto than allegro

Never the less, it was a symphony

I shivered down my spine,

I squirted saliva in my jaws

My soul at last was satisfied

My heart in me rejoiced

Breathtaking, life had come to me

in just that simple tune

I looked to the familiar tree, then to the sky above

to get a glimpse of the angelic chic

But she chose to be elusive,

And just when fortune smiled upon me

And heaven's joy I knew

She resisted the laws of gravity

I strained my eyes to see

But my heart danced with pleasure,

And I whistled her tune long after she was gone.

By Derrick Harding.

The Power Of The Cross

You may try to destroy the cross

You may burn it, blow it up , or shred it , you name it.

But you cannot destroy the power there of;

Things may not appear as you think they should be

But, realize there is no reasonable alternative,

For the mystery and the power of the cross

Truth and love are mutually exclusive and full of tension

But we must disciple with gentle firmness

You must strive to strike a balance

You must treat all men with dignity and self-respect

Integrity and ethical standards must permeate your decisions

Without judgment and love them into the kingdom

Racial justice anti-Semitism may raise their ugly head

But we must remember He whom we serve is bigger and

more powerful than the most deadly sin

Therefore, remember you are preaching righteousness

From a perfect gospel to a hostile world.

By Derrick Harding

The Spirit Lives On

If you stumble in life, your path grows dark

God's perfect will some evil hides,

And human frailty the worse for wear

Has weaken and wrinkle, till your body wanes

Let not your spirit in likeness fray,

Glow in thoughts, mature in wisdom,

And remain always, a youth at heart

Then day by day renew your mind

The sheen was seen on Moses face, when he descended

Mount Sinai's trace,

Shall be but dim when thus compared,

Then you shall prove, dreams come true,for God's Spirit lives in you.

Derrick Harding

The Splendor Falls

Adapted By: Alfred Lord Tennison 1809-1892

The splendor falls on castle walls
And snowy summits old in story;
The long light shakes across the lakes,
And the wild cataract leaps in glory.
Blow, bugle, blow, set the wild echoes flying,
Blow, bugle; answer, echoes, dying, dying, dying.

O, hark, O, hear! how thin and clear,
And thinner, clearer, farther going!
O, sweet and far from cliff and scar
The horns of Elfland faintly blowing!
Blow, let us hear the purple glens replying,
Blow, bugles; answer, echoes, dying, dying, dying.

O love, they die in yon rich sky,
They faint on hill or field or river;
Our echoes roll from soul to soul,
And grow forever and forever.
Blow, bugle, blow, set the wild echoes flying,
And answer, echoes, answer, dying, dying, dying.

The Real Story Of Mama

No one knows her true story

even you, may not believe it,

Some times I find it hard as well

In fact some of us don't even know her real name

She is Mama, Mum-ma, Mummy, Nana, Auntie,

Miss B, Miss May, and even Bess- Bess.

And with a touch of youthful idiocy, she's

The old girl or my old lady-

That wrenches some thing within my guts

For the truth I must have to ask; who on earth is that?

Then the facts speak, he is 12 and she is at the ripe age of 24.

The tragedy of the heart, robs innocence and subverts destiny

That, only Mama will tell,

For from her twelfth birthday she lived for him.

Yet, in this lies the mystery

Mama, she is universal

Her tears still fall, for dreams in her bosom

She has been to the school of hard knocks

Yes, those tears that soak her counterpane

When hell tries to break her will

She wraps her sullen eyes and weep

Yet this Mama, sets the tone too

For she's the main character in the saga of life,

She shows kindness, love, and courage under stress

And, by nature, for whatever standard you measure,

The journey she travels, tells her incredible story.

For me she lives; for us she dies

So we can be the who we are.

But stories are sure, they will not die-

Stories that we cannot dispute

For as long as the world shall ever last, the story

of Mama, half not told, will prevail for

all eternity.

By Derrick Harding

Time To Fight Back

I'd scarcely crave for earthly means,
But, thank the Lord I am redeemed
Unlimited wealth is on my mind
I bless the Lord for heaven's dream

For one day sure, this mortal soul
Shall march unshackled and cocksure,
The militant church in warfare mood,
Shall take back what is rightly theirs
That Satan hoards in storehouse strong
Defiant and boasting far too long.

And what joy that we shall share
With Jesus Christ our Savior near
The hungry souls He'll satisfy
With matchless blessings of grace divine
Then we shall worship endlessly
Jehovah Lord my Righteousness.

By derrick Harding

Too Late

It is the fullness of time
The former rain has come and gone
The latter now in torrent bursts,
And joyful hearts expectant wait
And flagging heads exalt and rise
to hear them testify and sing
For willing or unwilling, men must move
to plow, and sow and prophesy
Now reaping is their pride and joy
Trees and fields rejoice to hear
Their greenest banners they boldly wave
The glorious King towers supreme
A highway graced the desert floor
Valleys raise and exalt themselves
The mountains surrender their majesty
Rugged ways smooth themselves
No crooked, defiled or drunkards stride
To the way of holiness they all confide
All sprightly, nimble, youthful feet
trip and dance delightfully
Hearts that are purged and washed till white
sing triumphant songs of the redeemed

But, Alas! The cry that pierces the air
Is that of one for mercy cry?
The procession stops. I see him weep
But mercy's door closes shut.

By Derrick Harding

Tough Courage ...Tough Times

Strive on sister through pain and sorrow

Though your path darkness hides

Though life's mountain steeply raises

 confusion and dismay,

And your burden ne'er seems lighter, when

Your month comes to an end

Stay on course and reach your target

There is joy your mind can see

And the brave will know the difference

When this journey is complete.

By Derrick Harding

I Spill My Guts

This moment I remember well

And ah, what lesson I recall

My tears so hot comes streaming, down

my defiant face

And in that very moment, I spill my guts

I tell my complete story

I never flinch or wink

It foams, erupts and gushes

Thick lava of smut and shame

It oozes from my conscience

My sin like lava flows

It was the truth that matters, as I vent my grief to Him

This fearsome tale expels, as Jesus light comes in,

And my soul untarnished finds

The cleansing peace of Christ abounds.

By Derrick Harding

Wait For Your Promise

Don't neglect the seed that is within you
That promise is your baby
Though the answer may delay
And your faith may sometimes stray
The enemy knocks you flat, while you war,
You wait and hope;
You may slide and prostrate fall
You suffer many bruises
But this seed is your baby
Do not abort the sacred vision
Dare you suffer that still birth,
Do not have a gory miscarriage.
You may age and wrinkle and gray
Your spirit will blossom and stay,
Remember Sari and Abraham of old
You may be buffeted by family or foe
Remember Job the ever faithful
When your cross is too heavy to bear
For your joy is ever near
Remember Jesus our Immortal example
When He staggers up Golgotha's hill
He falls, the whip cracks,
Can you see the agony in His eyes?

Can you hear the whip across His back?

Remember you are on His mind,

Remember it is for me.

It is for you He dies.

So my friends keep the promise strong

Travail, for deliverance will come

Go ahead, shed your tears; for your tears of sorrow

tonight will become tears of joy tomorrow.

By Derrick Harding

What Is Life?

He is just a knee-high lad
His teacher tall; and straight and strict
She loudly sang, to his delight
with voice from way up in the skies
Life is but a little dream
And he, a captive in her class
Recalls her dint of gust and toil
No one dares by jest or will,
Opposes this, her sacred art
Desks and benches placate her wrath
When she draws near or flings that stare,
Slams them, wake up, sit up back straight
She drives in him the fear of God
So he by reason, strict comply,
To avoid the next unfailing lash
And though not clear, he hears her still
The words now only a bitter sweet
For life becomes a mountain trail
With unknown caverns and precipice steep,
They dread and fear no longer heap;
For Jesus by his side still keeps
That if he fails, he gently speaks,
To him who delights in heaven's reply
How soft, yet clear, so gently sweet,
Like the music of his thankful heart.

By Derrick Harding

Where He Leads

My life has come a full circle,
The link is now complete
And I am poised just on the edge
'Am ready for the journey ahead
Another phase, another light that signals full alert
This sterling purpose of my call, must guide me
to the next,
And where the path leads, I do not know
Therefore, I have no choice but one, to follow this
unbending course, where reality is but faith conceived
That I may glory in Christ alone and through my life
His glory shines, to direct lives on treacherous seas
to refuge through the Savior's love
And this by urgent quest I go, my hand in his I follow on
For going the way the Shepherd leads is far safer
than any man I know.
Feb. 14/04

By Derrick Harding

Who Is Mad

The deceiving image slips away

Every time she draws near,

From mirage to mirage she follows her

Hand akimbo, she pauses

She wipes perspiration from her brows

Her face steams in the midday sun

The callous concrete challenges her gaze

She searches the pavement, but it denies her quest

Curious onlookers carelessly laugh

But why can't they?

The mirror of life deceives so many of us

At least the hobo, as one shouts, shows her need and intent

Yet those laugh,

Why? Have they not heard?

It was by default that they are not on the receiving end?

By Derrick Harding

Rough Diamonds

Just beyond human's approval lurks
The precious salvage of heaven's joy,
I see them as diamonds in the rough,
Chosen from the unexplained,
They are rugged, coarse, and unkempt -
paupers, thugs and daring thieves,
Though camouflage by man's perception,
Classified, labeled and ready rejected.
Yet they await their balmy sunburst:
Rescued by God's redemptive plan,
The plan that changes rags for riches;
That transforms man from sin to grace
They move from nothingness to stardom
by the power of the spoken word.